# My Cat and Me

by John Serrano

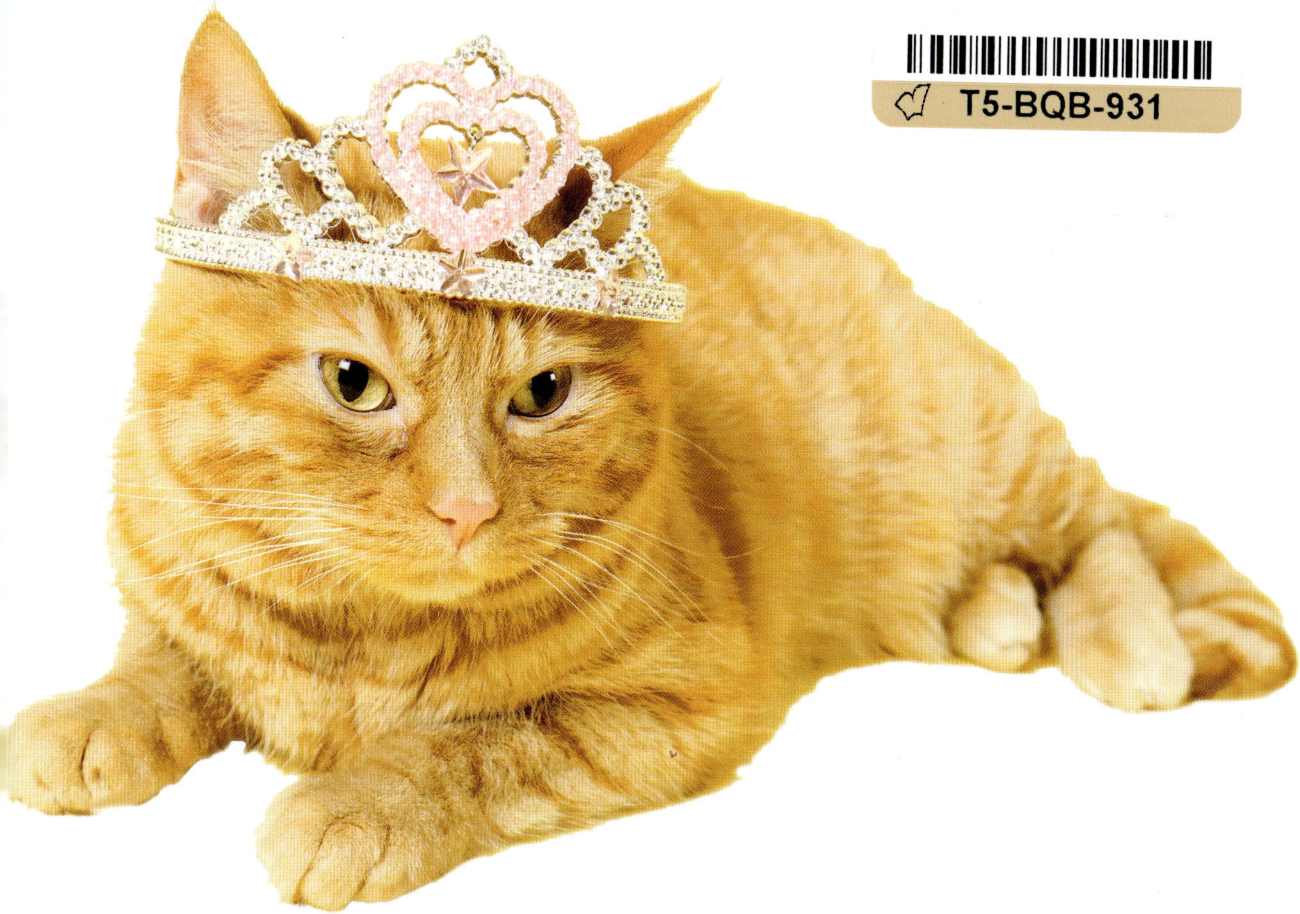

My cat has a bed.

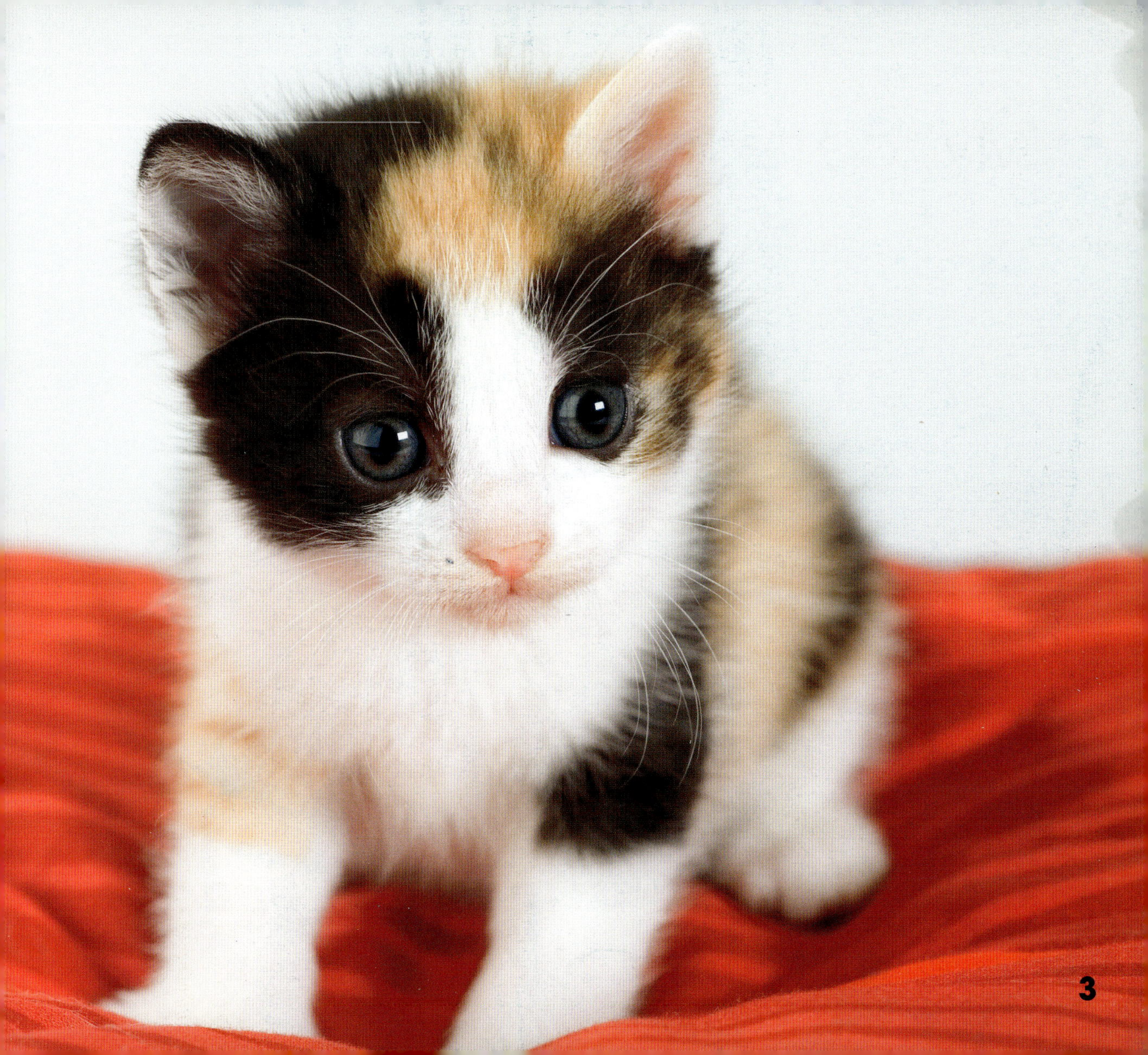

My cat has a bear.

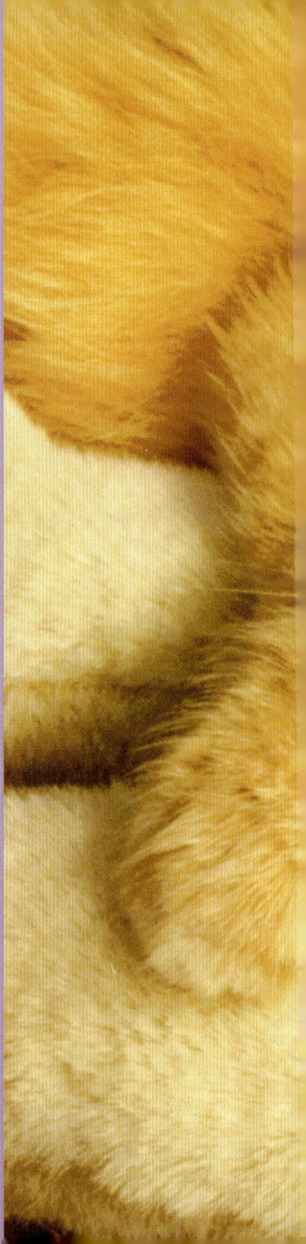

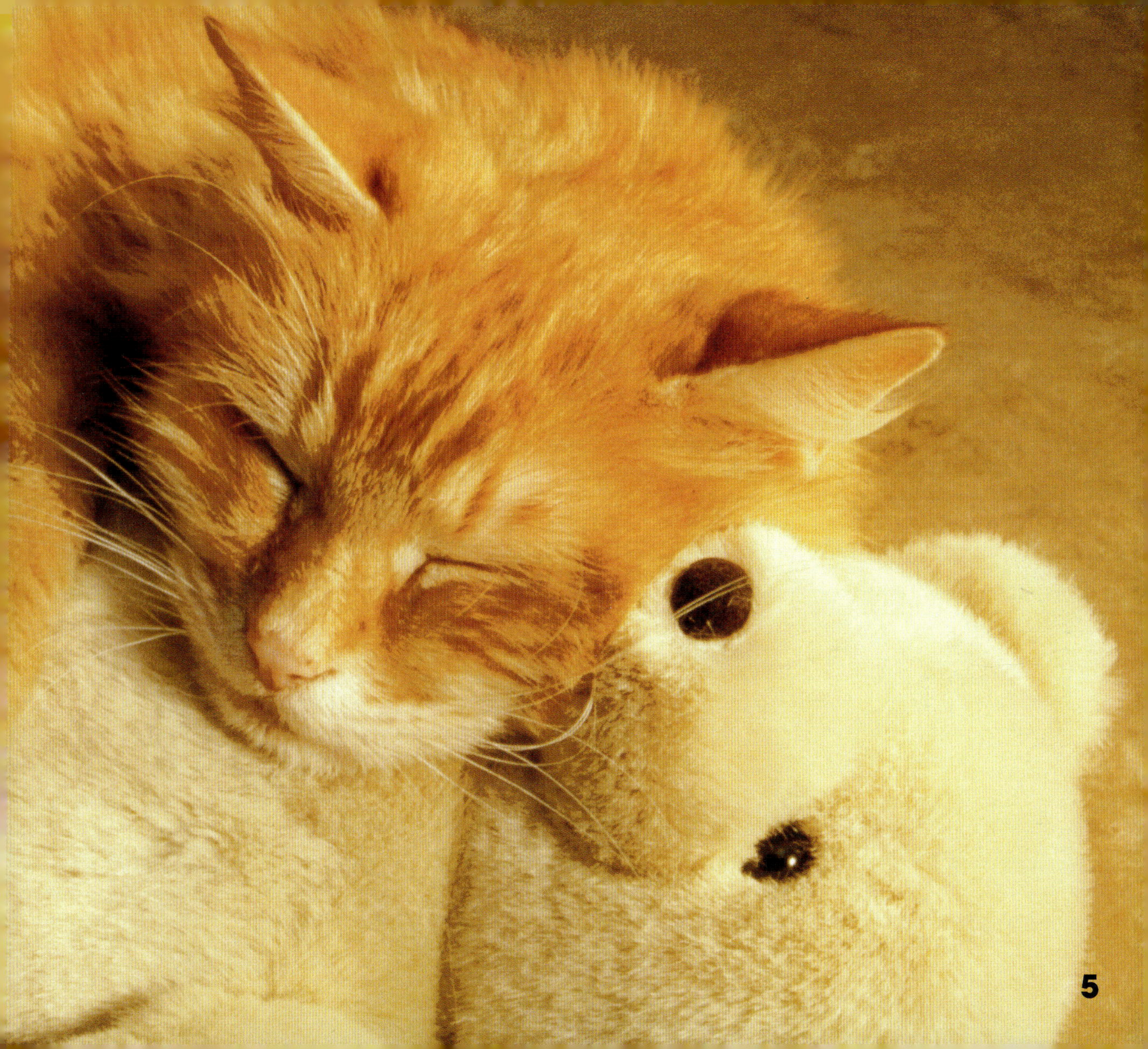

My cat has food.

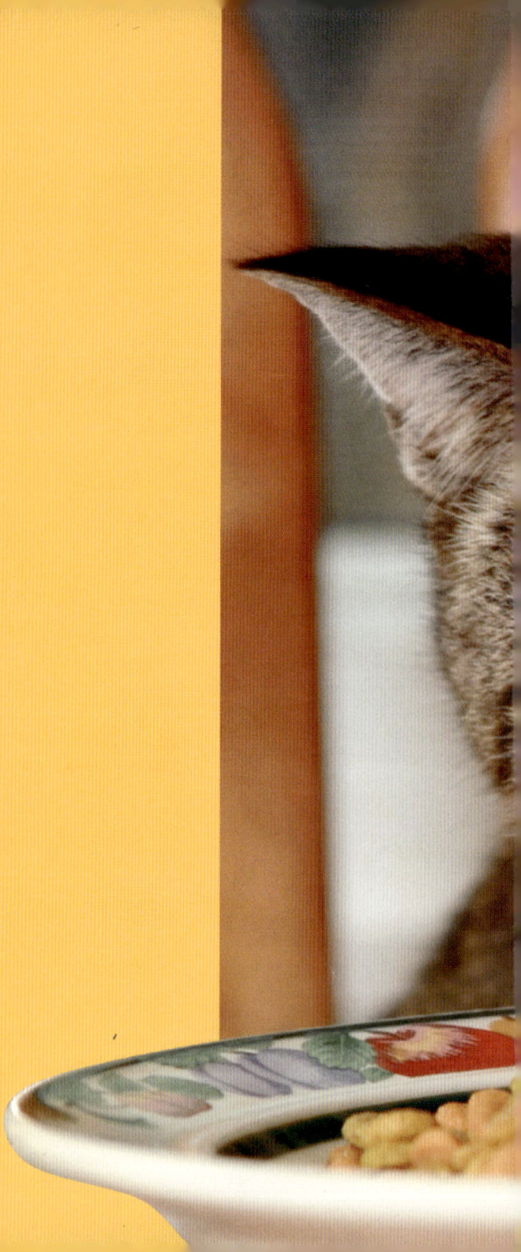

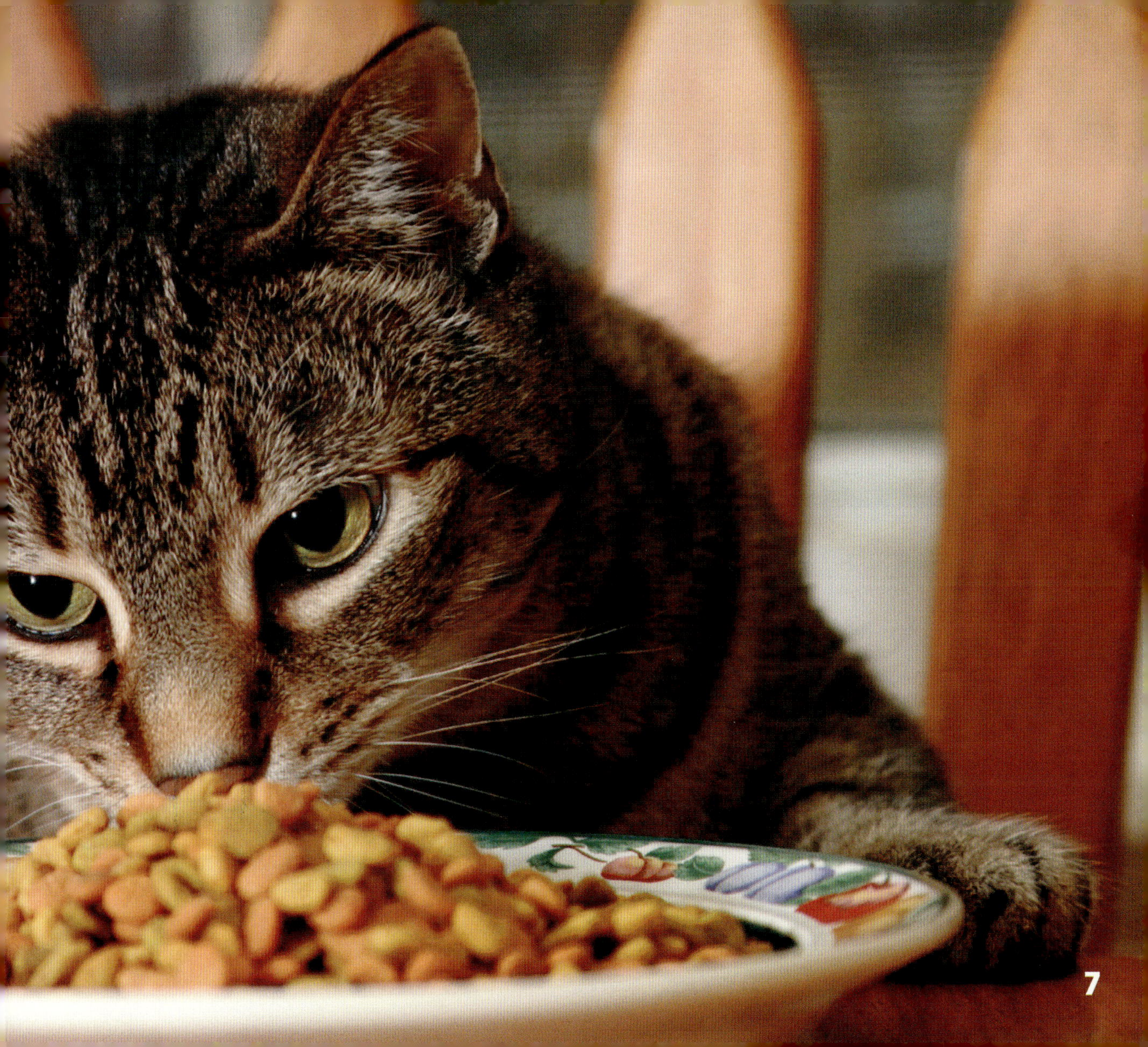

My cat has milk.

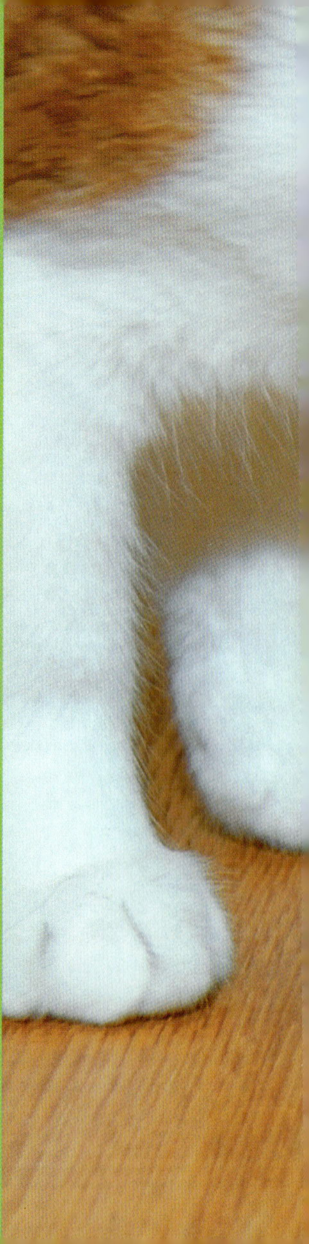

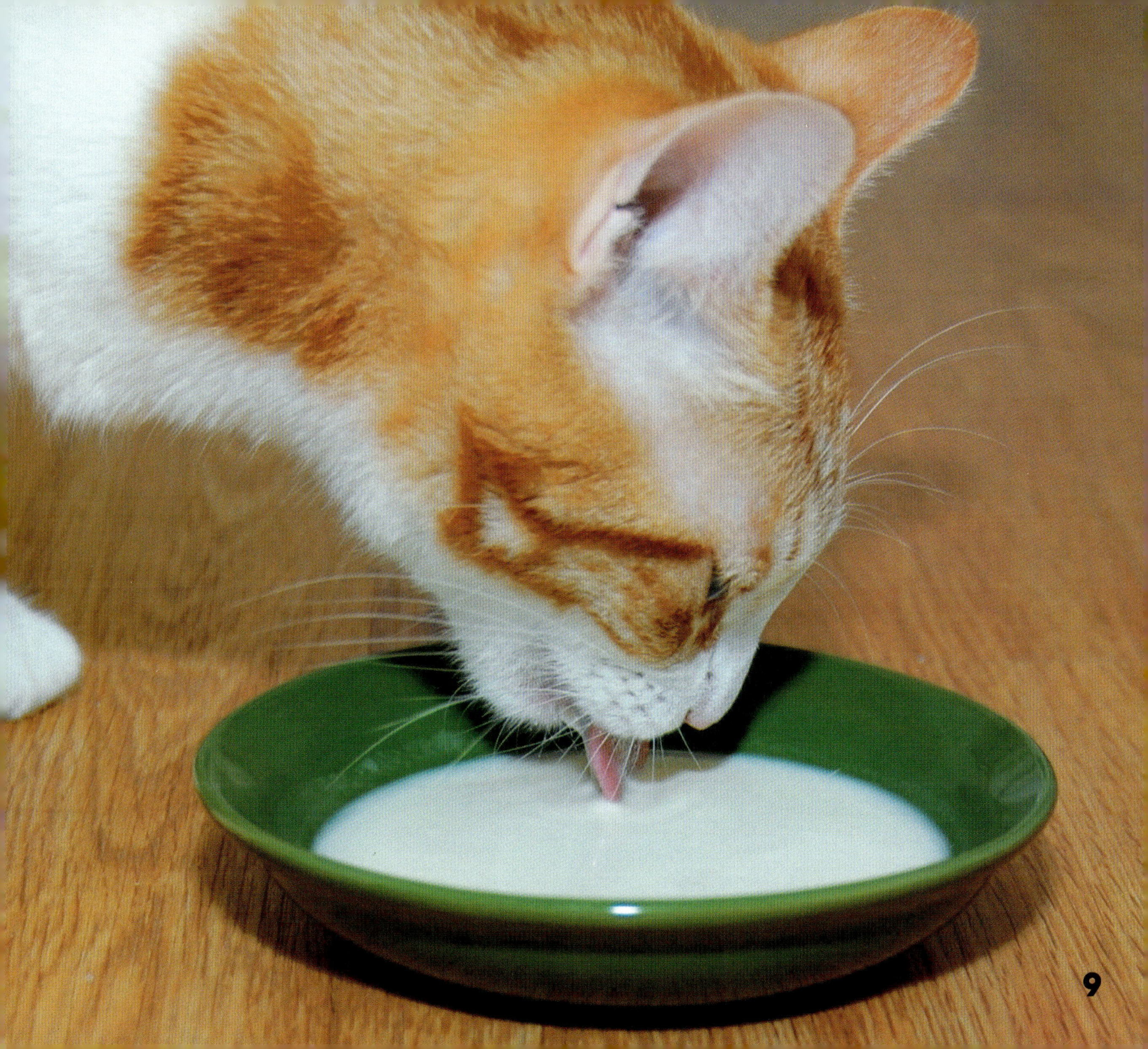

My cat has a ball.

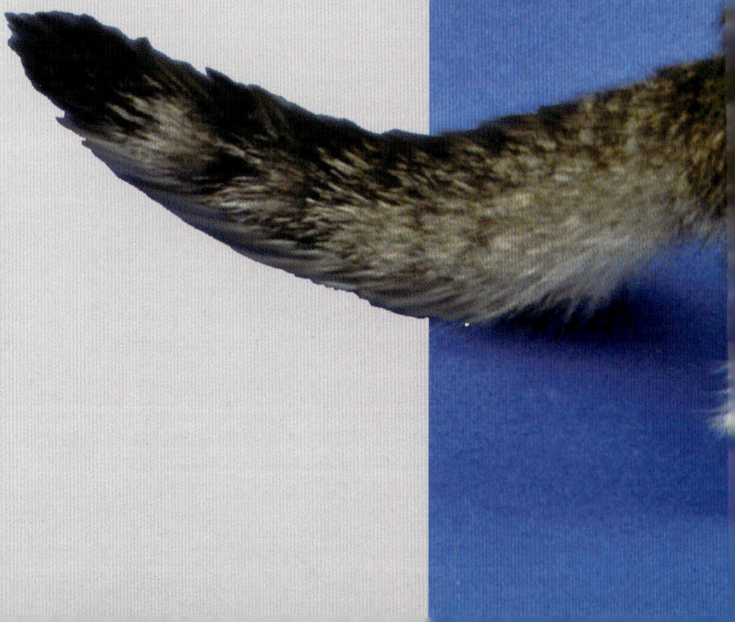

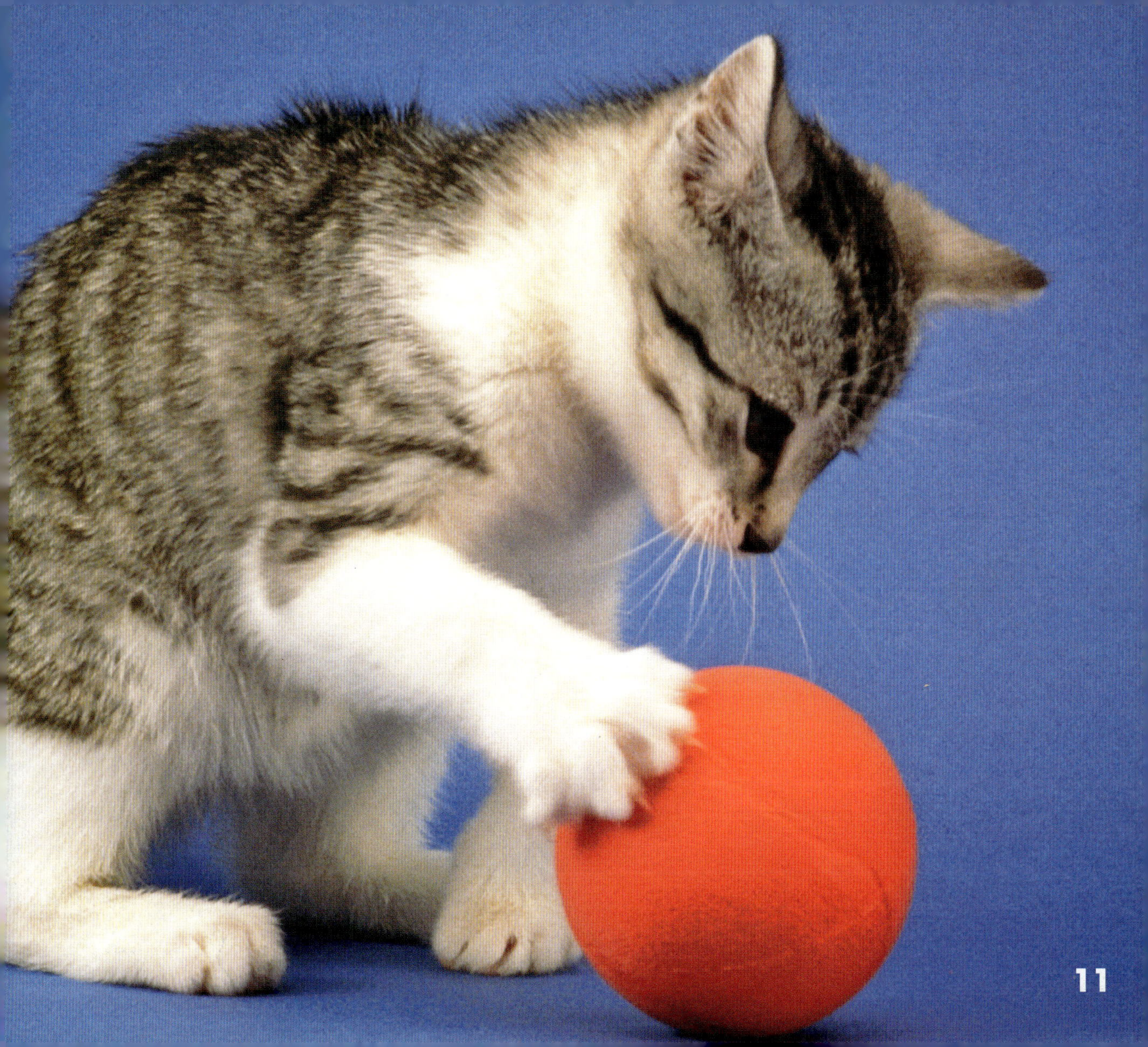

My cat has a mouse.

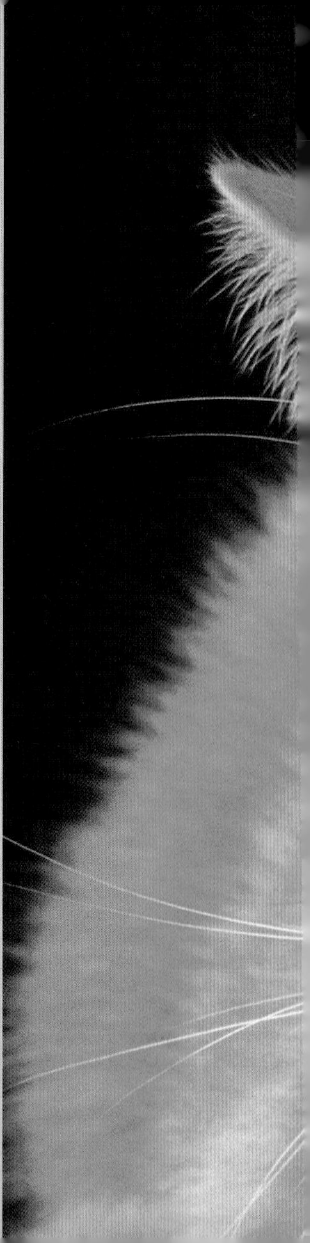

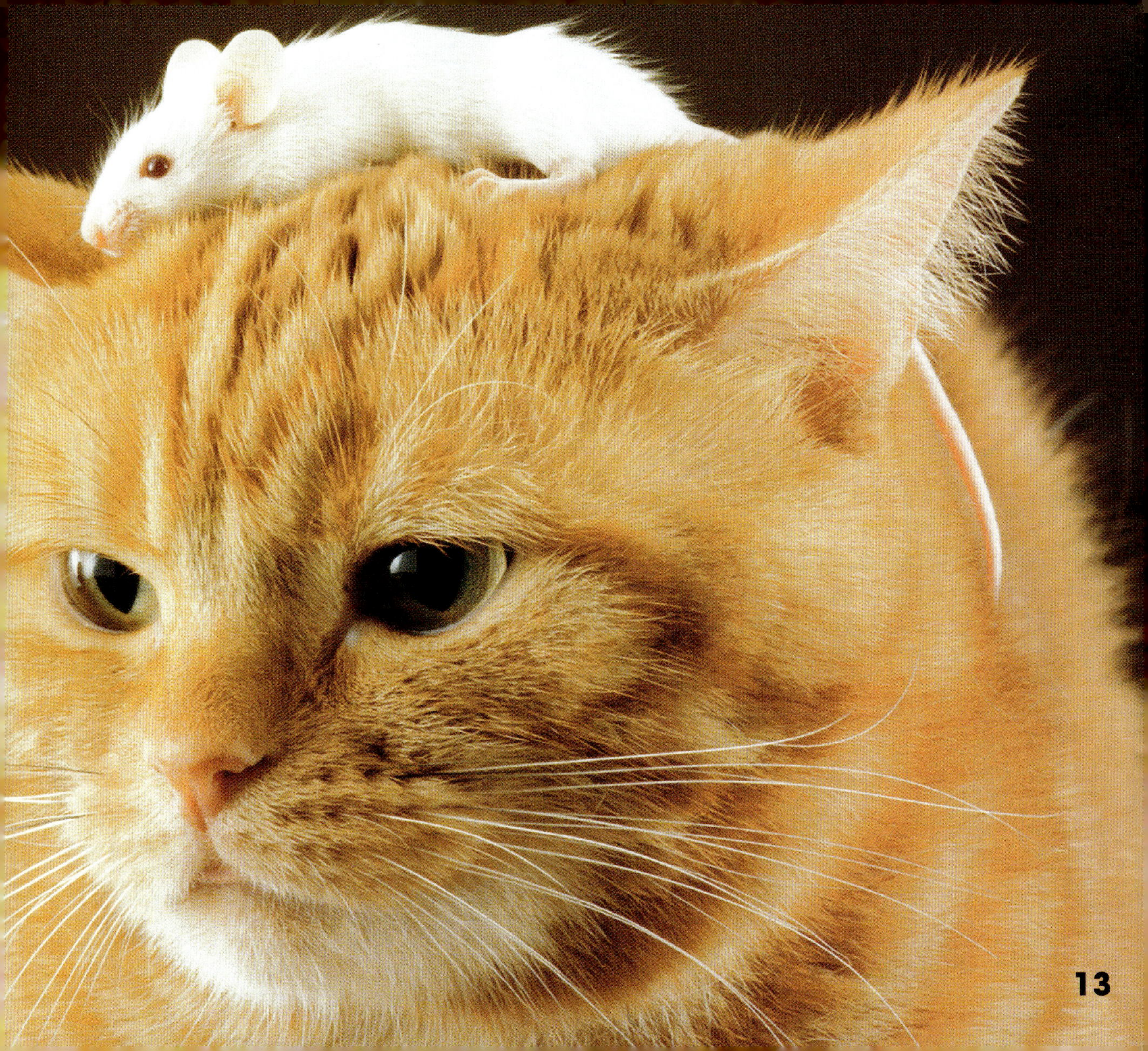

My cat has a collar.

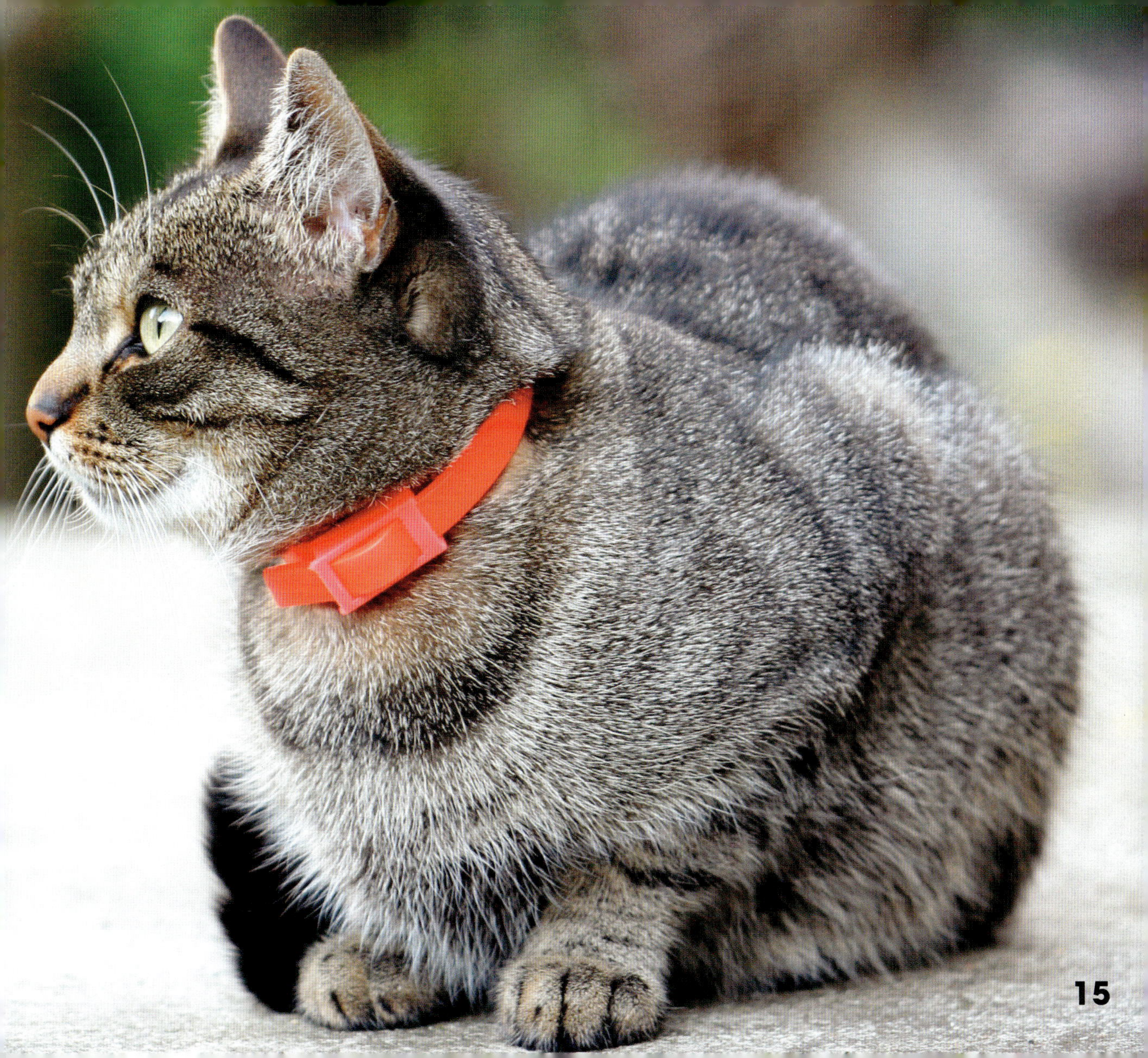

My cat has me.

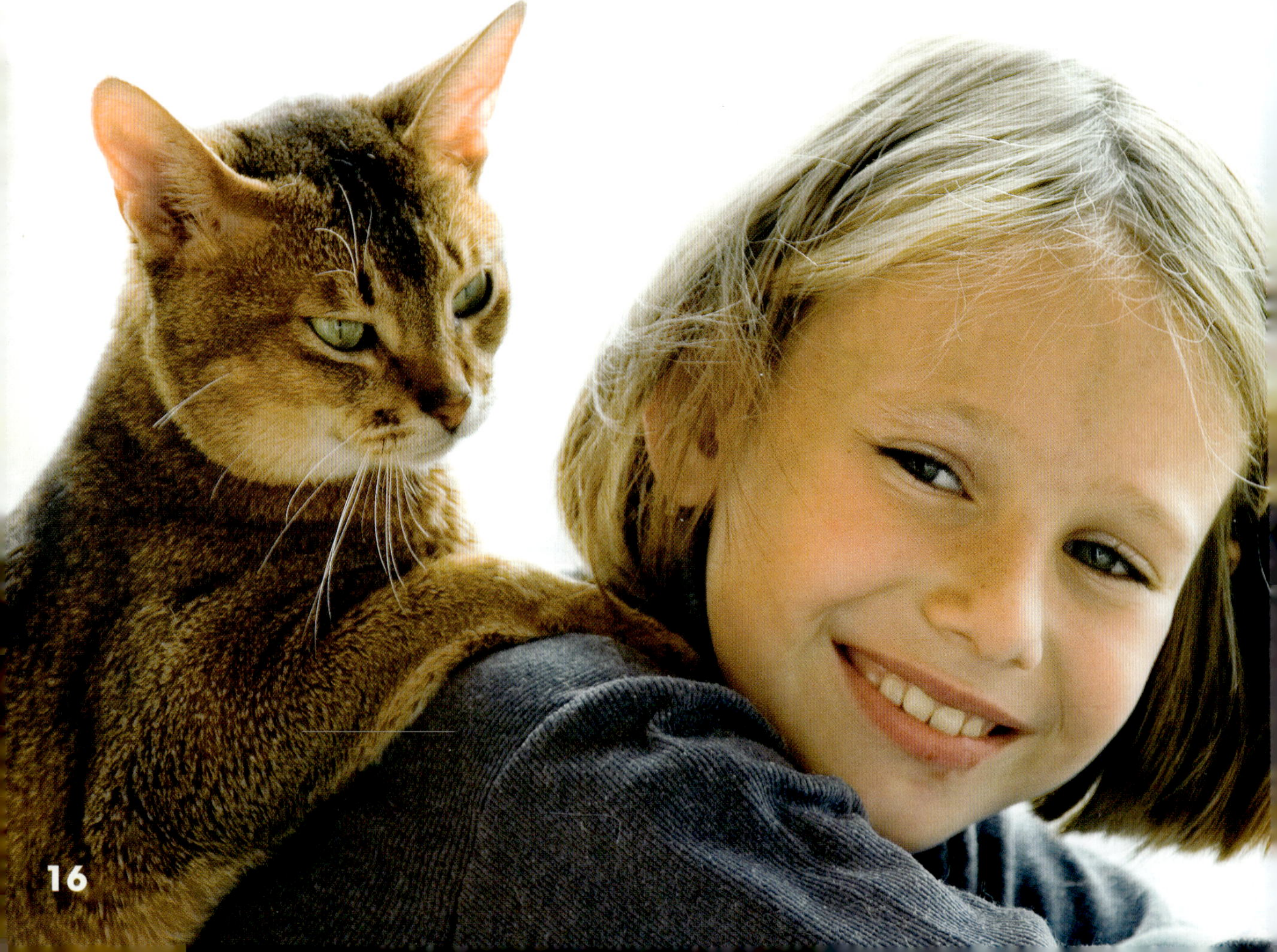